te st   ad l

WORK DONE RIGHT

Camino del Sol
A Latina and Latino Literary Series

WORK DONE RIGHT

poetry by
David Dominguez

THE UNIVERSITY OF ARIZONA PRESS   TUCSON

The University of Arizona Press
First Printing
∞ This book is printed on acid-free, archival-quality paper
Manufactured in the United States of America

08 07 06 05 04 03   6 5 4 3 2 1

Library of Congress Cataloging-in-Publication Data

Dominguez, David, 1971-
  Work done right : poetry / by David Dominguez.
    p. cm. — (Camino del sol)
  ISBN 0-8165-2266-9 (pbk. : alk. paper)
  1. Mexican Americans—Poetry. 2. California—Poetry. 3. Young men—Poetry.
  4. Sausages—Poetry. I. Title. II. Series.
  PS3604.O625 W67 2003
  811'.6—dc21   2002007373

British Library Cataloguing-in-Publication Data
A catalogue record for this book is available from the British Library

Publication of this book is made possible in part by the proceeds of a permanent endowment
created with the assistance of a Challenge Grant from the National Endowment for the
Humanities, a federal agency.

For Mom and Dad, who let me climb,
and Aaron, who knows,
y para mi Alma

CONTENTS

ACKNOWLEDGMENTS

I'd like to thank several friends who generously read this manuscript and offered suggestions: David Borofka, Frank Gaspar, Juan Felipe Herrera, Lawson Inada, Rick Rawnsley, Michael Spurgeon, and Franchesca Velazquez.

Also, my heartfelt thanks to Gary Soto.

My thanks to the editors of the following publications in which earlier versions of these poems first appeared: *El Andar,* "Lament for the Nopales"; *Crab Orchard Review,* "Club Las Palmas" and "Walking to Work at Dawn"; *Marcoli Sausage* (the Chicano Chapbook Series), "Between Magnolia and Ash," "La Historia," "Arizona," "Pig," "Contigo," "Ox Tail Stew," and "Chilalengua"; *How Much Earth, The Fresno Poets,* "Chilalengua" and "Highway 99"; *Bloomsbury Review,* "Cebu"; and *Solo,* "The Strike" and "Grinding Pork."

I will bless you abundantly and make your descendents as countless as the stars.—Genesis 22:17

WORK DONE RIGHT

Between Magnolia and Ash

I am Abraham, the great-grandson of Alberto,
  a Mexican soldier who crouched
below a shrub of honey mesquite and buried his uniform.
  That morning, clean sheets slapped
shoots of sun in the breeze,
  coals boiled laundry water,
and Rosa leaned over an aloe to massage
  her blistered wrist, and in her gray eyes a stillness
built on stones and leaves.
  In the yellow blooms, a tarantula hawk
sucked nectar above Alberto
  watching the insect body sheen deep
as a shotgun barrel in the sun,
  and he stroked water, stroked the wheat-colored sand,
and Alberto knew Pancho Villa approached.

  When Pancho Villa was only a boy,
he came in from the fields to eat
  and found his sister raped on a white tile floor
that grew dark as she squeezed
  her knees and became a point of dim light
in the lost bead of a green chandelier.
  His first bullet took the estate owner's thigh.
The second blew away his chest.
  The man felt nothing, and he leaned
his cheek on a window and saw
  a spotted wren look from the bones
of a cholla cactus and then died.

  Alberto brushed along the striated muscle
of a mare's hind legs, combed the black stockings,
  and picked manure from the hooves.
Perhaps, Alberto hoped, Villa would want the horses instead.

Alberto feared dust and imagined
Villa's men on palominos whose hides
   were spurred raw below the ribs.
Pancho Villa rode in the blue evening light
   that made the hard crags of hills soft.
Villa's Dorados surrounded the stables,
   dragged Alberto under a cottonwood, and tied a noose.
A Dorado took off his boots
   and soothed his blisters in the trough
and watched Rosa fall on her knees and wrap
   both arms around Villa's shins.
Perhaps the Dorado, as his feet cooled,
   when he didn't feel grains of dust
in the pink discs of broken blisters,
   perhaps it was then when he saw the sudden break
of Rosa's hip and waist and how it hung in the air
   so still he began to want her,
and perhaps it was then when Villa said, "No."

   Rosa and Alberto crossed the Rio Grande
and walked between the magnolia and ash.
   The starless sky held Rosa and Alberto,
the ranch behind them was no longer their own.
   They brought their blood, a cart,
and one young mare that twitched its ears and began to sigh.

PART ONE

I
Mi Historia

My red pickup choked on burnt oil
as I drove down Highway 99.
In wind-tattered garbage bags
I had packed my whole life:
two pairs of jeans, a few T-shirts,
and a pair of work boots.
My truck needed work, and through
the blue smoke rising from under the hood,
I saw almond orchards, plums,
the raisins spread out on paper trays,
and acres of Mendota cotton my mother picked as a child.

My mother crawled through the furrows
and plucked cotton balls that filled
the burlap sack she dragged,
shoulder-slung, through dried-up bolls,
husks, weevils, dirt clods,
and dust that filled the air with thirst.
But when she grew tired,
she slept on her mother's burlap,
stuffed thick as a mattress,
and Grandma dragged her over the land
where time was told by the setting sun....

History cried out to me from the earth,
in the scream of starling flight,
and pounded at the hulls of seeds to be set free.
History licked the asphalt with rubber,
sighed in the windows of abandoned barns,
slumped in the wind-blasted palms,
groaned in the heat, and whispered its soft curses.

I wanted my own history—not the earth's,
nor the history of blood, nor of memory,
and not the job found for me at Galdini Sausage.
I sought my own—a new bruise to throb hard
as the asphalt that pounded the chassis of my truck.

II
Galdini Sausage

Galdini Sausage sat on Sixth Street
      of industrial Del Sol marked by railroad and concrete.
            The front office and production
filled a cul-de-sac that opened
      its mouth to swallow gulps of wind
            blowing over the nopal orchard across Sixth.
The wind carried toward Highway 99,
      one great arm of overpass,
            off-ramp, on-ramp, cracked asphalt,
construction, iron girdle,
      one great arm desperate to hold
            some soft mercy in the dark.
The cul-de-sac sidewalk
      was lined by a long strip of grass,
            and every ten feet a Japanese maple
offered thin shade and a place to eat lunch.
      The workers walked out,
            not with the green hard hat nor with
the white smock of their work,
      not in pork blood, nor with pork fat
            wedged under their fingernails,
but clean, and they hung their gear
      in the warehouse, in lockers
            outside the bathroom where
they combed, rinsed vinegar from their eyes,
      and rolled down their denim sleeves
            when it was time to sit and eat.
On Fridays, the men crossed the street
      and took out pocketknives.
            Cherry wood and bone-burned handles
held the steel blades, and on the cutting edge,
      delicate as a dream,

the strokes of a whetting stone left like
the feathers on a quill.
        The workers walked around
            the nopal orchard and searched
for the plants growing outside
        the hip-high chain-link fence,
            squatted in Del Sol's summer heat,
swiped clean their knife blades,
        and cut the flat green nopales
            for weekend evening barbecues.
Most days, the men saved their strength
        with words under the trees at lunch.
            "I'm going down the highway,
and I'll have a small piece of earth and raise
        gray Appaloosas and palominos."
            The workers listened, and they knew.
And they stared beyond the nopales
        at the 99 leaving industrial Del Sol,
            and they took themselves
to other places behind their eyelids
        while resting in the grass
            under the green leaves of the maple.

III
Pig

I pulled into Galdini Sausage at noon.
The workers walked out of production
and swatted away the flies desperate for pork.
Pork gripped the men and was everywhere,
in the form of blood, in the form of fat,
and in pink meat stuck to the workers' shoes.
Outside, eighty-pound boxes of pork
melted under the sun, and as the sun worked,
the blood and fat grew soft, and the boxes,
lined with wax, became like thin paper soaked in oil.
Mack trucks came in with unprocessed pork
and took out chorizo, linguica, hot links, and sausage:
German, Sweet, Breakfast, Hot, and Mild.
One man stood straight up into the sky,
closed his eyes, and with his thumb and forefinger,
worked out bits of meat from his eyelashes
glistening like black grease under the sun.
The air conditioner in Mr. Galdini's office
made the papers from his desk float onto the floor.
He gave me a hard hat, a smock, an apron, and a hair net.
"You're in there," he said and lifted the blinds
of a window that partitioned his office from production.
He stood, gut pushed out, and his whole body
swayed with ease as we watched the workers walk out,
humpbacked under the unyielding memory of pig.

IV
Contigo

Outside the production room by dawn,
I waited to begin new work with strange men,
men who wore smocks, aprons,
hair nets, hard hats, and leaned,
chins tucked, arms folded,
and shoulders squeezed to block out
the sun for just a few minutes more.
The men laughed, talked, and breathed so carefully
there was a silence about them, a waiting silence I had yet to learn.

But from some far off place the men woke up.
They heard an engine rumble
and squeaky brake shoes.
"Mamas is here. Time to work," and Mamas,
short, heavy, and always on time,
slammed shut the big door
of her metallic gold Monte Carlo,
vinyl top greased to shine,
chrome bumper, studs and spokes,
and four shoe-polish-black whitewall tires.

Inside the production room, the grinder,
mixer, stuffer, and wrapper groaned
as the men took to their stations
and ground hundreds of cartons of pork.
The workers boated the sausage
and sent the boxes off to Country Girl,
Centennial Groceries, Food King,
and Little Henrietta's Deli & Bakery.

In one corner, Mamas taught me how to work.
"Just cut the links apart

and drop 'em in the tub," she said.
"Don't slash the casings
or we hafta throw 'em out,
but if you want, save one for a snack."

Mamas could work hot links for hours.
I watched the old woman,
liver spots and wrinkles deep,
and her fingernails, filed,
polished, and painted lavender,
flashed with silver scissors.
I slipped and slashed the links,
mangled them, dropped them,
cut the casings short, and stuffed
my pockets full of mistakes.
"Woman's work," I convinced myself.
And as my nicked-up knuckles
began to burn and fray with blood,
I watched Mamas move her hands with grace.

And soon I remembered the slender hands
of another woman who did
another kind of work I also watched.
She would stand at the stove,
over an iron *comal,* and roast tomato,
garlic, and jalapeño peppers.
And when the skins became so brown
and brittle they began to peel,
she made *salsa en el molcajete* so that
what I loved could plant and grow in the back of my throat.

It was the taste of my grandfather who sat
in the backyard under the pecan,
and it was the *el toro* tattoo
on his forearm I always asked to see,

it was the taste of a flatbed truck
and the piñatas and the tissue ripping free.
It was the taste of a brown paper bag
from Cielo's Bakery and the pumpkin empanadas
that warmed my palms, and it was the taste
of a long slow dance when the *tríos* played in the background....

    Tus besos se llegaron a recrear
    aquí en mi boca...
    "First tomatoes," she said as she worked,
    Llenando de ilusión y de pasión
    mi vida loca...
    "Peel them and then use the stone,"
    Las horas más felices de mi amor
    fueron contigo...
    "Carefully," she said, and she guided my hand under hers,
    Por eso es que mi alma siempre extraña
    el dulce alivio...
    "Now the roasted garlic," she said as she ground the cloves,
    Te puedo yo jurar ante un altar
    mi amor sincero...
    "Now the jalapeños,"
    A todo el mundo le puedes contar
    que sí te quiero...
    "Then mix them together with the stone,"
    Tus labios me enseñaron a sentir
    lo que es ternura...
    And she put *salsa del molcajete* on my tongue,
    Y no me cansaré de bendecir
    tanta dulzura...

I tasted a narrow creek and the current
that flowed around smooth stones,
the way she parted her hair

and the curls that wrapped behind her ears.
I tasted her brown skin, and it was
a Mexican brown, rich and powerful like a river that would not stop.

V
Hornworms

My spine was limp the morning
I put my head on the conveyor belt of the wrapper
and slept while the men loaded the rollers with new spools of plastic.
I dreamed about a tomato garden
where I searched for trails of excrement
left by hornworms fat as sausage: a chorus of larvae
that filled my ears with their jaws
when I leaned over the vines and listened.
I watched the pulse of their torso and dared myself to anger
their horned rears into the raised brows of gods
who created moons out of leaves.
The fresh eggs lay hidden,
pupae already slept buried in the earth,
and the hummingbird moth would glide above
the naked trees come winter,
but these masters of work were mine.
With a stick, I peeled them off the vines.
I felt their frantic eyes, dropped them in dirt,
and twisted the toe of my boot.

VI
Grinding Pork

I lifted a box off a two-thousand-pound pallet of shoulder,
    stripped the cardboard,
        then heaved the block into the meat grinder.
The grinder banged against the floor,
    and I feared if I turned my back,
        the grinder would tip over and blindside my head.
At the bottom of the grinder,
    ground pork filled a bin I gave to Guillermo,
        who dropped the pork into the mixer.
He added spices, vinegar, and water,
    and rolled the pork to the sausage stuffers.
        "We're falling behind," Guillermo said, "go faster."
Guillermo grabbed a carton
    and tossed the pork block into the grinder.
        "Watch out," he said.
He cracked two more cartons across his knee,
    pushed each block through the blades,
        and mixed the batch.
This was my first day grinding pork,
    and I watched the crew,
        men who rolled up their sleeves
and worked themselves into a sweat in a freezer.
    "Production starts with me," I said.
        I threw up a box,
ripped away the cardboard before the pork hit the grinder,
    and when I finished a pallet,
        I called for more pork.
The crew saw that I had caught up,
    that I had lined up the bins for the mixer,
        but when the fat became packed
in the treads of my work boots,
    I slipped, and my head slammed against the grinder.

Unfamiliar with this work,
I understood not how the men
returned each morning with nothing
but sleep in their eyes:
I understood that I was grinding pork
at six o'clock in the morning,
that I was tired and cold, and that I felt
a knot on the back of my head that made my legs weak.
Guillermo helped me up and said,
"Ándale, we still have three hours until break."

VII
Fingers

Because of the frozen meat and a silver ring,
my index finger swelled and dimmed.
The men held down my wrist and used a saw.
I fought back the need to squirm and watched
where the nicked-up teeth missed
and the scars began to form.
I remember the day Julio longed to go home.
Nothing passed time like work,
unconscious work when the bones pounded
and the muscles stretched.
So when the stuffer jammed, Julio jumped on a stool,
lowered half his body into the machine,
and when his thigh brushed against the go button,
the blade moved an inch
and sliced off his index finger.
I wiped up the blood and thought about Julio,
how he did not cry out,
how he asked for my smock
and held his hand against his chest,
how he pushed away those who tried to help.
How the finger was never found.
But most of all, I thought about myself:
would I have screamed, could I have taken the pain,
walked outside to the employee pay phone,
and, with my good hand still held steady, dialed 9-1-1?

VIII
Cebu

The pork Mr. Galdini told us to use was no good.
Mold grew along the edges of the cartons,
and the melted pork smelled bad.
Miguel lifted a box, cracked it across his knee,
used his hands to guide the scraps into the mixer,
and as the blades ground the meat,
the rotten smell of pork poured into the room.
Miguel gagged hard, and he covered his mouth,
his whole body writhing like some beast
had ripped out the muscles of work.
"Let me help you," I said, "I'll mix the meat."
Miguel stopped his work and looked into my eyes
as if searching for stars of a land he once knew.
"I'll pay you," he said, "marry my daughter.
She is very pretty, but still in the Philippines."
And in the frozen production room,
with his callused hands floating down like
the brown magnolia leaves in fall,
against the stench of blood and bad pork,
Miguel traced a young woman's warm body.

IX
The Cactus Orchard

Guillermo and I searched for stray nopales that ripened
outside the fence into a sweetness
we ate *con carne, salsa de tomatillo,* and homemade tortillas,
a sweetness we washed down
with cold beer Friday evenings
after our work at Galdini Sausage was done.
Kneeling over a withered nopal,
Guillermo wiped his brow and said,
"The most famous person
I ever met was Bette Davis, I fixed her car once."
We watched starlings dive under telephone wires,
come back around and perch,
then swoop in a slick of oil and disappear
like the dreams that vanish
when you wake at dawn for work.
In his hands, Guillermo weighed
the dried-up nopal, dropped it into the dust,
and looked toward Highway 99.
"I'd like to be someone else today," he said,
and he spit at the pig blood
on his work boots and dragged them through
the dead orchard's dirt.

X
Leaving Home

That morning, I worked in the garage with my father.

We took crowbars and broke down the shelf he built
for my bedroom when I was a boy.
We piled the scraps in the corner to make room for other things,
and we kneeled in the sunlight,
over the sawdust, and picked out the nails
still straight enough to use.

"Your mother says take the truck," he said,
and he pointed at the dead robin
on the floor under the window, where the shelf had been.

The beak was cracked, only the torn cobwebs
that floated like light
looked as soft as the feathers
soothing the ants who worked slowly in the heat.
I put on work gloves,
my father opened a paper bag,
I felt the robin's weight in my palms,
and I stared through the window at the flowerpot
hung from the eaves.
I recognized this robin … a robin my mother loved
because it returned each year
even after the cat got wise
and sprang up and tipped the pot and licked
the spilled eggs off the cement.
The robin watched from the telephone lines,
sang into the night, and when the sprinklers turned off,
she came down and drank
from the grass.

I could see Galdini Sausage from the bus stop at Horizon Park.
For ten hours I had scrubbed
the boat trays and the carts where the pork was kept.
I scrubbed until
the steel wool dissolved and my skin
felt wrung from a rag above a bucket of gray water.
Behind me, in the trees,
the birds sang louder than even the traffic.
A bus could have taken me back to my youth,
back to the familiar hiding place
behind the sumac along the side of the house,
but that wouldn't be right.
I longed for my red truck, a tank of gas, a tailwind,
and for the eucalyptus along the 99
sloughing down to their skin for the stars.

XI
Red Pickup Truck

The mechanic thought he had fixed it all,
and he told me I had new
gaskets, filters, and spark plugs,
a new carburetor that hummed like a kitten,
and the cooling system,
caked with gunk and the worse he'd ever seen
in twenty-three years of professional work
as a professional mechanic,
had been flushed out all night.
The mechanic pointed his wrench at the sun,
took off his baseball cap,
wiped his brow with his sleeve, and sighed.
"But we won't know," he said,
"in this heat, and I'm just sayin' so you know,
until you drive that truck hard."

I didn't ask because I didn't want to know.
I wanted to drive and after fifty miles
stop and call Galdini Sausage, say I quit,
then drive on toward Yosemite
and the white dogwoods drooped
over soft rotten logs where I'd sit and ask
the cross-shaped blooms for their perennial secrets.

I took it easy at first and cruised down the 99 in fourth gear.
The windows were cranked open, and on the radio,
loud, desperate, and raspy,
the Beatles sang, "Don't let me down."
And I screamed—screamed lyrics formed in my gut,
screamed until my throat burned,
screamed until the lyrics filled the cab like wind
pushing the truck afloat across the 99.

I saw the currents of the San Joaquin River rolling along,
and the long road was also smooth.
I hit the foothills and popped down to third,
climbed on up, and the mountains,
at once clear and distinct,
stretched their backs against all I hoped to forget.
But on the flats, while at sixty in fifth,
the oil dropped like blood and rose in plumes of blue smoke.
I drove one mile more than I knew I should
and coasted off the highway as the engine shut down.
For the second time in my life,
I knew just where I was—stranded in the parking lot
of a bar called El Gato Triste.

In the back of my truck, I had a carton from Galdini Sausage.
I sat on the front bumper, ripped the box open,
and scooped up two links of chorizo.
I stared at the links and hoped the chorizo would reveal
my future like a handful of bones.
But in the Del Sol heat, the casings exploded
and filled my palms with an ooze of pork
that burned beyond the nicked-up knuckles of work.

PART TWO

I
Rise Like a Moon above Industrial Del Sol

At the edge of the nopal orchard,
Guillermo nailed an iron stake into the ground.
He took forty strides and hammered home a second.
Friday morning, and we had finished
our work at the factory early.
Guillermo spit into his hand, pitched a horseshoe,
and leaned the shoe against the stake.
Guillermo believed the orchard was still good,
that the seasons had left more
than dust under our boots.
"Like this," he told me, and he rolled dirt
and bits of weeds into his palms and pitched another.
The orange iron arched high,
landed, flopped over, and raised a plume of dust.
Across the street, the taco truck
made its routine stop at the employee parking lot.
I bought two black coffees in paper cups,
burritos wrapped in wax paper,
and I shared breakfast in the orchard with my friend.
Guillermo finished his burrito and said,
"I'm sure the nopales will grow."
Guillermo took out his knife, sliced off a yellow nopal,
scooped out a few handfuls of dirt,
planted the nopal three inches deep,
and the nopal held like a moon above the earth.
Earlier that morning, Guillermo asked me to help him
trim a pallet of meat in the freezer.
Guillermo, a man who came to work on time,
a man who always smelled like
aftershave and the lotion he used to comb his hair,
sat swearing in perfect Spanish because
our smocks hadn't been washed

and because the smocks smelled like
the glands and stomach we used to process chorizo.
Guillermo and I opened a carton.
We took out chunks of pork, trimmed away the mold,
and tossed the chunks into a bin.
Even with the mold trimmed, the pork felt slimy,
and we talked about other things to avoid the smell.
He wanted to sit on his porch with
a basket of nopales and a knife to pinch the thorns.
Guillermo said, "And I like tossing irons along the river."
We finished the pallet in silence,
morning moved slowly toward noon, and when
the pallet was empty, we clocked out,
and tried to leave our thoughts of pork for some other day.

II
Club Las Palmas

Open vats of red vinegar fermented outside:
108° of Del Sol heat and black asphalt.
Guillermo and I choked on the vinegar's vapor
as we threw cardboard boxes,
still ripe with scraps of guts, into the dumpster.
Pig blood poured from the boxes,
ran under my smock, and down my skin.
"This is no way to live," I told Guillermo.
Guillermo dipped his hand
into a box lined with wax,
used his hand like a wooden ladle,
filled his palm with warm blood,
and he held it very still as if
blood might reveal lost memory
or a life that he had yet to live.
At noon, we ate lunch.
Flies, maddened by raw meat,
stuck to our skin and dizzied the air,
but I still heard, splitting industrial Del Sol,
the freeway where I wanted to be.

I wanted an age too young to remember,
when fog settled across the Valley and my grandfather,
who drove trucks for Ringsby Rocket,
passed by on the 99 and took
the Jensen off-ramp to check in his emptied rig.
At home, he put his soft-bristled wooden brush beside the towel
smelling of shower and shave,
and he sat to eat nopales and chicken
my grandmother sweetened with red chili sauce.
He slipped into the black silk-lined coat
of his best black suit, and opened

the black case of his trumpet,
and after each valve was oiled,
and after the floral-carved bell was polished,
we drove to Club Las Palmas,
and Abraham's Latin Combo began to tune.

At Galdini Sausage, lunch was over.

Guillermo fixed his collar with dignity,
and he undid his belt, and his pants
with dignity, and he pulled out his shirt,
and he pointed at the rope-thick
purple scar sagging hip to hip below his belly
where he once cut himself open
to let out the life he did not want.
"It is better to work," he said, and tucked in his shirt.

Have you seen a man give himself to this place?

Guillermo and I started a pallet of Sweet.
We ground shoulder and cartons of fat.
We added molasses, sugar, and anise,
then sank in beyond knuckle and elbow
and pushed it all through.

III
Oxtail Stew

At five o'clock in morning,
I walked to work and passed the green ponds
of Horizon Park where the last bluegill,
caught on the low, slight bank,
panted hard in dark mud, crushed glass,
sour bottle caps, whiskey,
and the iron weight of heat and smog.
This haze stared through eyes
gray as the broken window panes
on the cheap side of town,
and when this haze held you
and whispered in your ears its quiet tragedies,
it stole your breath quick as time.
This is where men gathered to sell peanuts,
buckets of oranges, and roses,
and they sat on the benches and watched
the trucks drive by and disappear.

What I want to say is simple:
a man must do more than sell roses
where the bums go and beg—
he must keep something holy.
He must breathe the winds
that rustle the orchards of the valley
where the white almond blooms
replenish with their soft scent.
He must learn from the Appaloosa
when she walks in from the fields
and bows her head to a trough of water
that reflects nothing but her eyes and the stars.

Shoulder, fat, bone, and loose sheet metal
banged out a day-long cacophony.

Twenty-eight pounds of spice
had to be mixed before the grinder was done.
Mustard powder, paprika, salt,
and chili powder boiled in my nose,
in my eyes, and in the red throb
of my hard nicked-up knuckles.
By late morning the meat defrosted,
and the boxes began their ooze.
Pig parts became easy to recognize.
Eighty pounds of guts, kidneys,
and stomach fell across my chest
each time a box ripped apart.
We dared not stop the music of our work:
the clack of a clean pine pallet,
pink meat and white fat ground to a pulp,
sweetened, stuffed, and crimped,
the chorizo boxed, the boxes labeled,
stacked, and wrapped.

At lunch, I watched Guillermo hunker over the table
and dig into his stew—carrots, potatoes,
celery, oxtail, and gravy, made from
chili peppers and fat, smoldering in a ceramic bowl.
Guillermo took out a white cotton napkin
and spread it evenly across his lap,
picked up a piece of sourdough ripped
from a loaf and soaked the bread in the stew
for a long time . . . his own tired body
taking back what the work took, and he ate.
He sucked on chili peppers the color of blood
and took another bite of the bread.
He sucked out the beef from the eyes of the bones
and gnawed on the soft marrow,
and he drank hot coffee sweetened *con canela.*
"Eloisa," he said, "can cook," and he touched

the brown lace crocheted into the edge
of his cotton napkin, rubbed his gut, wiped the table,
and walked out to complete his work.

IV
Lament for the Nopales

The equipment pushed through before dawn.
We watched from across Sixth Street.
We watched how the chain-link fence
was wrenched free and rolled into spools.
We watched the bulldozer
crawl over the curb and lower its teeth
into the ground until the roots
popped like the bones of the dead.
We watched the orchard
rise in the dust under the street lamps
still glowing at this hour.
We watched the flatbed pickups roll in,
and we watched them unload
the Port-a-Potties where the shade
collected like a pond.
We watched the dumpsters
fill up quick, and we watched
the boom of the crane stand silent against
the sunrise, the trailer trucks,
and the steel beams that came in on trains.
We saw the mixers pour cement
across the dead dirt of Del Sol,
and we watched the heavy slab take shape
where the orchard once grew.
These days we hungered for more than memory:
these days we longed for the orchard,
the last spot of industrial Del Sol
where the dust was the dust of the earth,
the dust that settled on our brow,
mixed with sweat, and left on our handkerchiefs
swipes the color of clay, those days,
when after work we sat on milk cans

in a circle of shade and good conversation
at the edge of the orchard to peel
the skin and thorns with a quick pocketknife blade
until all that remained was the bright green meat of the nopales.

V
Overtime

We rocked from foot to foot on rubber mats.
Guillermo dipped fifty-inch casings
in a bowl of warm water and salt.
Five racks had to be filled, and on each rack,
forty-eight linguica had to be hung.
Guillermo bent back his head and stared
at the florescent lights of the factory
and then asked, "What happens when you die?"
We stuffed and crimped, a casing split,
and the meat filled the endless day like a gush of blood.

VI
The Strike

Under a Japanese maple to eat lunch with the crew,
Guillermo explained how last week
he worked overtime, how large plates of glass
had been replaced and that Mr. Galdini
refused to pay the Concord Glass Co.'s disposal fee.
How he had to pile the discarded glass
beside the dumpsters, how the half-inch-thick plates,
even with their smooth, green edges,
cut with silent ease into his palms until
the heavy glass reflected the color of blood,
like the stained windows in church.

The crew sat down in the damp shade,
and Miguel, as if he found honor in the silence of death,
slept on the lawn with a flower over his heart.
"¡Levántese viejo! You're not dead yet!" yelled Guillermo.
"Do you know what we need?" he asked. *"Una huelga."*
The workers looked up and inched away,
and their eyes zigzagged across the factory like
the crazed flies above the dumpsters.
Guillermo, from the pit of his muscled throat,
in a tone soft and deliberate, said one word, *"Huelga,"*
and again, *"Huelga,"* and again, *"Huelga,"*
until the word raised the crew off the grass,
and they bent their knees and found
a rhythm lost in the work of blood and meat,
and the word took hold of their collars,
and the word dripped in the beads of sweat
across their brow, and the word began
to beat and pump like a fist . . .

HUELga, HUELga, HUELga, HUELga.

Mr. Galdini finished eating lunch in his office
and leaned out the window, listened,
sliced his leftover sausage,
stuck toothpicks in the penny-size bits,
and walked outside with a pink tray to offer
his leftover links as their lunch.
Mr. Galdini squeezed Miguel's shoulder.
The crew became silent, a hymn
lost in the pews of an empty church,
and as Guillermo watched without words,
the men took the toothpicks,
raised their hands to salute Mr. Galdini,
and swallowed the sausage.

VII
Chilalengua

I dreamed they gave the JFK Peace Prize to an empty chair
for exposing the horrific oppression of
the Chilalenguan government upon its workers.
The chair was lovely: fine mahogany, a green cushion,
and a silk banner draped like
a humanitarian bridge across the armrests.
How useful the morning paper was.
Earwigs, with only a few bits of meat for food,
took weapons and maneuvered
across the production room toward freedom.
A thick club of newsprint stopped them dead.
Their crisp insect corpses became
immobile pinches that dotted the concrete floor
close to that safe spot behind the wall.
Obituaries marked where the dogs slept.
They dreamed of other things,
the warm corner of a couch and a master's
kind odor that lulled them to sleep.
These thoughts alone were a risk, so the dogs
remained obedient and silent to avoid the winter night.
In Chilalengua the weather was fine.
Long rows of skulls baked under the sun.
Their large black orbitals dotted the fields of sorghum.
One skull with a cracked cranium wouldn't keep its mouth shut.

VIII
Mamas

My grandfather repaired the railroad near Oleander.
Forty years of shoulder and spine.
Far down the tracks, he'd pause,
and dusk would push through with a silence
that humbled the open earth.
He hammered hundreds of spikes each day
until one evening when a sliver of iron,
the shape and size of his own
fingernail clippings, caught him in the eye
the way the moon's claw snags
those who are alone and lost in the night.

The morning Mamas was late to work,
the men sat worried on the hoods of their cars.
On a white bicycle with fat tires,
Mamas rode up to the curb of the factory,
slid off her comfortable saddle,
planted both feet on the ground,
and her blond bouffant stood a defiant posture
against the crows that swooped so high,
the men looked like mice out from a rock.
Back straight, arms cocked, Mamas
stood ready to launch two fists and gathered
a gulp of breath, "Stop callin' me 'Mamas.' *Soy Victoria.*"

The crew winced at one another and prepared for work.
Mamas, her tongue against the pallet of her mouth,
her voice more bold than the scar
that blinded my grandfather's eye, began to peddle off,
one knee rising above the other,
the body's healing grace after the work is done.
"I quit," she said, and slowly rolled away.

IX
Psalm for the Dark

Guillermo and I sat on the curb and sipped coffee at dawn.
The gardeners drove by in trucks loaded with sacks
of manure and trays of blooms bright enough to garland the dead.
The morning remained so calm, we felt one with the earth.
We sat on the curb and stared at the 99.
We longed for more than making sausage in Del Sol.
Across Sixth, the boom of a crane
towered twice the height of the street lamps,
and we knew soon the highway
would disappear behind the smoke stacks
and the haze of another new factory in Del Sol.
Guillermo brushed clean his black denim work shirt,
sharpened the crease of his jeans,
and ran his index finger under his thick mustache.
Guillermo said we'd buy a ranch.
We talked about sipping coffee at dawn on the porch,
and imagined the land where the Appaloosa
nuzzled alfalfa on the ground.
We saw the fog settle in the plum trees,
listened to the Ford Ferguson
turn the soil at the furrow's edge, and the sparrows,
who were unafraid, ate the worms.
At night, only the stars and the moon for the light.
Guillermo and I finished our coffee.
The sun rose, and the steel frame of the new factory
dropped shadows on Sixth: let the shadows punish,
but let the earth rise again and again.

X
Highway 99

For a fresh carton of Galdini German Sausage
     and for a silver thermos of black coffee,
        the crane operator agreed to lift Guillermo
     high above the cracked asphalt of Sixth Street,
high above Horizon Park,
     high above the new factory,
        high above even Galdini Sausage.
     Guillermo shed his bloody apron,
his cotton smock, his hair net,
     dropped his hard hat on the concrete slab,
        and stepped onto a plywood platform he and the operator rigged,
     gave two-thumbs-up,
and grabbed the thick cable of the crane.
     The crane operator pulled down two tight green-knobbed levers,
        and I watched Guillermo lift off the ground and sway in the breeze.

When I was six years old, I climbed the magnolia in my front yard
     because on Christopher Columbus Day
        the teacher said, "The world is round,"
     a confident declaration that found no home in my logic,
for even from the magnolia tree,
     the world looked flat as my hand.
        I scoured the city for the earth's arc,
     and when the tide of the night rose and then fell,
I continued the search because the stars guided wise men home.
     But while under the spell of the August evening,
        I discovered not the world's edge
     nor the terror of a thinly branched treetop
bending side to side like the masthead of a pilgrim ship.
     From the top of the magnolia,
        high as telephone poles along Sherman Street,
     amid the city yearning for more and more land,

I spotted the walls of Food King,
      Hart's Pharmacy, and Susan's Fabrics:
           the places I hated
      loomed only two blocks from my bedroom window.
I declared myself captain of a boat,
      a captain fit for a gold compass, the parched scrolls,
           and fit for the starboard side view of the evening earth
      when the blue water slept, and the magnolia blooms
filled my palms with the scent of lemon.

The end of an overtime shift dragged meat-heavy into Friday evening,
      and it touched the darkness that hides the dead.
           The dark reeked of blood and buried the men
      who filled their hearts with thoughts
of extra pay never worth an hour of the work,
      and the men sat slumped in their cars,
           and their dark heads were hung low, and their groaning was dark,
      and their tired, sour breath stank of the dark.
Guillermo, high in the air as the giant boom could reach,
      the white of his eyes alongside the white emerging moon,
           standing on the platform and scouring the city,
      holding his arms out like wings to balance his weight in the wind,
his mouth locked agape and his torso bobbing up and down,
      Guillermo, possessed by the force of creation,
           pointed at the sunset glowing down the highway,
a cement spine that left industrial Del Sol and throbbed with life.

XI
Your Name Is Abraham

I stood alone in the storage freezer.
The empty rigs waited bound for Merced,
Madera, Reedley, Selma, and Kingsburg.
I stacked boxes on the first pallet.
I thought about the day
my brother and I buried our red Guinea pig.
We planted a camellia over a shoe box
and let the water run from the hose.
Mud soaked through the patches sewn
into the knees of our jeans, and we stared at the sky.
I thought about the night my father,
when I cried in shame because I got beat up,
took me into the yard filled with the scent
of the jasmine crawling on the fence.
My father pointed the telescope at the sky,
told me to look up, and said,
"Your name is Abraham, father of all nations."
I wrapped the first batch in plastic,
loaded one ton onto a trailer with the forklift,
and killed the engine next to a stack of pallets.
For a moment, the factory rested quietly,
and I took off my leather work gloves
and stretched my arms toward the sky.

PART THREE

I
Walking to Work at Dawn

I lifted my fist, sniffed the pig blood in my knuckles,
and wondered what crevice of my body
the pork would claim as home.
I once watched a *curandera* in an orchard of figs,
her skin like the bark of an ash, save my friend Jesse.
We washed windows at the car wash.
He felt pain, coughed up blood,
and thought years of ammonia fumes
had settled in the folds of his gut
that only magic could reach with its sticks of mystery.
A fire burned under a ceramic pot.
The curandera added pinches of mint and cat's claw,
and then she stirred the water
the way branches sway until there is only wind:
a faith blue jays hold in their wings,
diving through the morning fog for fruit,
crying, "Squa, squa, squa, squa,"
just before the frozen ground slams home.

II
Road Trip

The afternoon filled the black streets of industrial Del Sol.
Outside the production room,
their faces soaked by overtime and sweat,
bent down at the waist
to scrub clean the chrome carts used to mix
paprika and pig guts for chorizo,
Julio and Miguel, clumps of fat
stuck to their skin, and, despite the heat,
in plastic aprons that dripped blood,
Julio and Miguel,
who volunteered to work late, looked up,
swiped clean their mouths,
and watched me and Guillermo clock out.
In the employee parking lot,
Guillermo and I dropped our gear—
the hard hat and hair net
on top of the apron, the apron on top of the smock,
each crumpled upon the other as if
we had left as the only mark of our lives
the blood, fat, stink, and spiced meat of pig.
Inside Guillermo's black van,
our T-shirts showed the sweat,
and we embraced the heat,
for this was not the heat of work,
this was the heat of a weekend road trip.
Down Sixth Street,
we threw up our arms and yelled like fools,
"¡México! ¡México! ¡México!"

III
Mexicali

See it in the monsoon winds
        that wrestle the night in the vacant lots.

In the *masa* slapped over the iron stoves
        where the women and the *chisme* are always happy.

In the eye of a dead crow crying out,
        "All life is delicate, all life is delicate."

At night, the wall disappears,
        and the lights on top look like stars.

A man finds it in his chest and drums,
        Boombababoombababoom, and his woman

sways her hips, *"Ándale,"* she says, *"ándale mi amor."*
        Make it yours, lean into the ocotillo,

and beyond the spikes and the petals of fire,
        below the surface of the desert and the black roots,

hold out your tongue and wait
        for the arched tail of the scorpion.

IV
La Paloma

In the patio at Las Palapas,
Guillermo and I sat to eat breakfast.
I watched Señora Paloma,
a woman with hair pulled into a bun,
each strand soft as feathers
rounding the crown of a dove.
She carried a tray of bowls
and a pail filled with ice and beer.
She took two dark bottles,
wiped away the ice with her palms,
squeezed lime around the edge of the mugs,
sprinkled the salt, and poured
the beer against the side of the mugs.
Next she put on the table
a bowl of lemon wedges,
and then a second bowl filled
with cilantro and onion,
then a bowl of dried oregano,
and at last jalapeño peppers.
La Señora wanted us to taste our food.
We sipped the menudo from deep bowls,
a rich and steaming pig's feet taste,
the tripe cooked so long,
it melted and sweetened the hominy.
Guillermo said, "All things can be cured,
and God cured the hangover
with hot bowls of red menudo."
On a stage in the patio, Los Caballeros
filled the air with trumpets, tuba,
clarinet, snare, and cymbals,
and the sunlight danced on their boots
and in the rivets of their jeans,

and the light settled in the folded brims
of their hats and dripped like
the water they drank to cure their thirst.
La Señora Paloma asked me, "Are you happy?"
I added more lime to my beer,
and my nicked-up knuckles burned.
Señora Paloma asked me again,
"Sir, are you happy," and I listened to her voice,
and it carried in the wind, and it settled
in the eaves under the palms of the new morning.

V
Let Nothing Lie Dormant

At the farmer's market in Rosarito, Mexico,
a man touched my arm.
He sat on a stool at a wooden table,
and in the center,
a blue pitcher of water beaded under the sun.
Hunkered over his lap,
he worked with a gouge on a block of walnut,
and he blew at the dust,
and the dust swirled in the breeze.

Done stripping the sapwood vulnerable to rot,
the man held the heart of the wood,
a purple wood hard against
the chisel's cutting edge.
He looked up from his work,
and his gray eyes told me I must listen.
"This wood must be strong
or the heart cracks before the real work is done.
See this?" he asked softly,
and he lifted a mallet carved
from a branch of apple, "Strong wood," he said.
"It wanted to be more than a tree."

He rubbed fresh walnut dust between his palms.
We drank glasses of ice water,
talked about life in general,
and he used the pitcher,
billowed and wet like the sail of a boat,
to cool his neck.

Later, through the soft meat of an avocado,
I felt the pit longing to be free.

VI
The Tovar Bull

Along the downtown sidewalks,
white guayaberas swung in the breeze.
I wanted a white one,
a white guayabera adorned with paisleys,
a white guayabera
that reminded me of my grandfather
who spent the afternoons
under the pecan tree of my backyard.
I'd sit on his lap,
and we'd listen to afternoon boxing on Spanish radio.
I remember the day we heard Joselito Bienvenida,
a boxer I cheered for because
he tattooed his children's names above his heart.
I remember closing my eyes
and the challenger's tassels that danced like fire
as Joselito's eyes swelled shut,
and when Joselito left himself on the ropes,
the beating began.
Joselito, out on his feet,
died in the ring.
My grandfather and I sat unable to speak
until he took from the breast pocket of his guayabera
a handkerchief that he knotted into
a mouse that jumped from his palms and glided
through the air—
white and filled with the sun.
We munched on *chicharrones* from Cielo's Bakery,
and when Grandpa used the handkerchief
to wipe my mouth,
a stream of light passed through the branches,
and I saw the scar in his eye,
a large white scar
like the ghosts floating through my dreams.

"We are Tovars," he told me, *"fuertes como toros."*
With the tip of my finger,
I traced the *el toro* tattoo on his forearm,
and he told me he saw a Tovar bull
kill the most promising matador in Mexico City.
The bull's neck muscle was so thick,
the matador couldn't push the sword down
and through the barrel of the chest.
The matador gave up
and tried to slice the bull's throat, but the bull,
hidden for a moment behind the cape,
went under the sword,
and pierced the man's groin with both horns.
The bull watched the blood
soak the dirt before other matadors chased it away,
and my grandfather remembered
the bull's black eyes
reflecting the sunlight even at dusk.
The white guayabera I tried on felt like
the skin of a guardian saint,
and I saw Joselito out on the canvas.
I thought about the bull, too,
how he went *under*
the sword and stared at the matador
after the matador was dead.
I looked into a mirror
and admired my white guayabera,
the hide of a bull
all ghosts would fear.

VII
El Ranchito

The stars above Mexicali shone brightest above the ranchos.

Along a ditch, Guillermo and I walked
where he had played as a child.

Guillermo held a pail, and he wanted
to fill the pail with milk for breakfast,
to scrape off the cream that rises,
and to spread the cream on toast.

We found an alfalfa field,
sat on top of railroad ties tacked with barbed wire,
and listened to the crickets and shooed away the gnats.

"I remember this field," Guillermo said.
"My father used to graze his cattle here."

Scouring the field for a cow to milk, Guillermo tsked
and said, "The cattle are gone, but maybe we'll see horses."

We followed the barbed-wire fence deeper into the night,
and in the corner of the field we found
a spotted blanket grazing near a well.

We sat down on a pair of railroad ties.
The pail hung from Guillermo's work boot,
the bottom of the pail reflected the stars,
and the horse ripped the grass from the earth and chewed.

At the well,
Guillermo filled his pail with dark water.

He walked up to the horse
and took her pink nose into his palm,

lifted the pail, wrapped his arm around her neck,
put his cheek on her shoulder,
and held the pail for the Appaloosa even after
his arm began to shake.

I watched Guillermo,

and I knew what a man sometimes longs to hold:
I knew why Guillermo gave the Appaloosa water.

How sometimes, under the stars rolling over barbed wire
toward another day of work, and yet another,
the only thing worth touching
is something of home gracious enough to say,
"Close your eyes now and sleep."

VIII
Encarnación

My friend and I sat on the fine white sands of the beach.
We built a small fire to roast nopales
and jalapeño peppers from the farmer's market.
I had a stack of corn tortillas wrapped
in pink butcher paper and two ice-cold bottles
of *horchata* in a Styrofoam cooler.
Guillermo roasted the jalapeño peppers.
He talked about our work at Galdini Sausage.
He most liked grinding the meat,
and he showed me how to crack open
the frozen boxes across my knee and to push the trim
through the grinder in one swift motion.
The nopales and the jalapeños hissed,
their roasted skins looked as brittle as my scabbed knuckles
that cracked and burned at work
each time I pushed pork through the grinder.
Guillermo sliced the nopales into strips that we put
in the tortillas, I added jalapeños,
we opened the horchata, we ate,
and the food was good, a sweet jalapeño burn
that burned nothing but our hunger and our talk of work.
I leaned back on my elbows
and stared at the blue waters rolling gently.
I saw, only slowly at first, the white cloak of healing,
afloat on the tops of the waves,
and that was when I told Guillermo, "Let's swim,"
but Guillermo lay asleep in the sand.
I stood, unbuttoned my guayabera, took off my boots,
jeans, socks, and charged the sea,
but the sea, as if to make me prove my faith,
knocked me down, and I breathed,
lifted my head from the sand, and then I was swimming.

The ocean touched my tongue and sank deep as
the pork in the pores of my skin.
I was alone between two waves,
afloat on my back in the palm of the Pacific,
and for a moment, because nothing else mattered,
I closed my eyes and listened:
water under the birds, the wind, I heard myself breathe,
and in my knuckles, I smelled only the salt.

IX

When the Machines Stopped at Galdini Sausage

Guillermo and I huddled around the time clock with the crew.
The morning, always brightening by this hour,
lay in haze and hung between the moon and the sun.
The smell of the nearby slaughterhouses
racked even the sausage factory,
and Guillermo swore he heard the cattle bellowing.
"I don't like the cry of a cow being slaughtered," he said.
Guillermo said his father once boiled
a cow head after he discovered that Guillermo was stealing
cans of evaporated milk from the pantry.
Guillermo, home from school,
found the skull tossed on the front porch.
Above the skull, steam rose,
and bits of cartilage clung to the long snout.
"It's your dog," his father said.

We punched in, and Guillermo gave me a slice of banana nut bread.
Guillermo wanted to grind the pork,
and he asked me to help him mix the batches.
The shoulder, fresh from the freezer,
choked the grinder unable to chop the frozen blocks into a pulp.
I dumped the pork into the mixer,
used my fingers to break apart the chunks,
and my hands turned pale blue.
Angry because of the dull grinder blades and because
the men teased that we worked too slow,
Guillermo pushed each block through
not with his fists but with a second block.
Guillermo worked like a man who, up before dawn,
read the paper over juice and toast, and then,
as he walked the empty streets
toward a factory that offered nothing,

realized there was nothing but work done right.
The grinder banged against the floor,
and top-heavy with the pork,
it tipped over and split open Guillermo's head.
Guillermo lay dead upon a pine pallet.
The men lifted the grinder and over the body
spread out a clean, white smock.
I picked up Guillermo's pocketknife,
the bone-burned handle and blade freshly polished,
and slipped it back into the sheath
Guillermo wore on his belt.

At the bus stop, I sipped a cup of coffee,
and the banana nut bread tasted good.
I stared at the sky for a long time and pictured
Highway 99 and my red pickup truck
that could take me on a journey I no longer longed to begin.
I thought about the afternoon Guillermo and I
went fishing at the San Joaquin River.
We sat on the bank, and as he baited his hook,
Guillermo hummed "La Paloma."
I baited my hook and told Guillermo about
my grandfather who fished with hotdogs
and died while singing "La Paloma" on his guitar.
At the church, I followed the coffin outside
and stared at the statue of St. Francis
soothing his palms like Christ in the sun.
I liked how St. Francis always nestled,
in the folds of his robe, white doves
who sang all through my grandfather's mass.
Guillermo pulled down the tip of his pole,
hooked the length of a night crawler,
and when Guillermo let the pole go,
the barbed hook ripped up his thumb.
Guillermo watched the blood run down his wrist
then cleaned the wound and cast the line.

"Tell them to bury me here," he said.
Guillermo liked the smell of cottonwood leaves
and how the tassels in the sunshine
floated through the air and never touched the ground,
and most of all, Guillermo liked how at night
the twigs became so stirred,
they turned into a song.

X
Elegy

Remember the workers of the factory
gathered in a circle at the edge of the nopal orchard;
remember the green limes Julio shared,
ask how he picked the limes from a tree in his yard
and polished them under his palm on his knee
until the fruit's oils rose to the surface of the peeling;
remember the *cahuamas* we drank,
how the bottles were wrapped in paper
so the beer stayed cold enough to enjoy after work;
remember how we stood side by side
and sang the old songs and made our throats burn;
and remember Mamas who brought to an orchard
in the center of industrial Del Sol a bowl
of mussels soaked in lemon, onion, chiles, and salt;
remember Guillermo who taught me how
to remove the thorns of the nopal with the meat untouched;
and remember Miguel standing among the workers
to honor *con un brindis* the week's forgiving, unenduring end.

XI
The Perseid Showers

I was behind the factory, as usual,
tossing heaps of garbage into the dumpsters,
 and when a soggy carton ripped,
pig blood soaked my new work boots.
 "I quit," I said and drove off.
That night, I parked on the cliffs above King's Lake,
 and the water reflected the clear night.
In the back of my red pickup,
 nothing but the stars, a place to sleep,
and my name: Abraham Tovar,
 a music that filled my ears …

    Abraham, father of nations,
        Tovar, a fighting bull.
    Abraham Tovar,
        great-grandson of Alberto
            but not the soldier who ran from Pancho Villa.
    Abraham Tovar,
        grandson of Marciano,
            but not the man who worked railroad for forty years.
    Abraham Tovar,
        nineteen years old
            and no longer up at dawn to work at Galdini Sausage.
    Abraham Tovar,
        father of nations and strong like a bull.

I drove down Covenant Road
into the foothills covered with wheat,
 and I heard the cottonwoods singing.
A stream fell from the mountains,
 and the stream left the valley
of my blood for the unsowed fields.

God said, "Look up at the sky
and count the stars, if you can."
I looked up at the sky and saw
the summer Perseids and the blood of will
alight in streams of rock and dust.
Stars white as doves filled my windshield,
and I found Highway 99, and my truck
hummed new-engine smooth.

ABOUT THE AUTHOR

David Dominguez was born and raised in Fresno, California. He was educated at California State University, Fresno, and the University of California, Irvine; received his MFA from the University of Arizona; and has attended the Bread Loaf Writer's Conference. His chapbook *Marcoli Sausage* was published by the Chicano Chapbook Series. He has also been published in various magazines and journals, such as *El Andar, Faultline, Flies Cockroaches and Poets, Crab Orchard Review, Luna, Bloomsbury Review,* and *Solo.* In addition, his poetry appears in the anthology *How Much Earth: The Fresno Poets.* He has taught at Long Beach City College and now teaches writing and literature at Reedley College in California's San Joaquin Valley.